The
Best
10 Minutes
of
Your Life

ZOE WHITTALL

McGilligan Books

Cataloguing in Publication Data

Whittall, Zoe
  The best 10 minutes of your life

Poems.
ISBN 1-894692-01-2

  I. Title. II. Title:Best ten minutes of your life.

PS8595.H4975B47 2001   C811'.6   C2001-902418-5
PR9199.4.W44B47 2001

Permissions:
The phrase "The Best 10 Minutes of Your Life" is copyright Kaia
Wilson from the song to be broadcast live performed by The
Butchies. Used with permission. All rights reserved. With
thanks to Bikini Kill for use of "rebel girl."
The poem Separate Bodies was previously published in Queen
Street Quarterly, July 2000.

Cover photo: Maureen Grant
Editing: Lillian Allen
Copy Editing: Noreen Shanahan
Layout & Design: Heather Guylar

McGilligan Books gratefully acknowledges the
support of the Canada Council and the
Ontario Book Publishing Tax Credit
for our publishing program.

The Canada Council | Le Conseil des Arts
       for the Arts | du Canada

Contents

Love letters to dead poets / 7

Someday this will be years ago / 39

This isn't stress, it's a shotgun / 65

Je me souviens / 93

For Willy Mudball Scott and Ange Holmes, aka *the Bitchin' Camaros*, because now it is years ago ...

Love letters to dead poets

Dear Gwendolyn MacEwen

I'm baking bread, turning words in wet flour:
warm breakfast for the stars.
kneading the velocity of fear.

T'is the season I can't connect
myself to the 6 year old
Polaroid girl in blue corduroys.
 I breathe into your pages
        (pink pumping lungs)
words that slow my own industrial panic
end my monologues of malaise.

I'm writing my autobiography
spoon scratches in the bottom of my bowl
        (green glass; bits of rice)
rush out to meet another girl who's trying
to stay out of the hospital
        (or just stay out of the way)
until thaw
wringing our hands of love and dyeing our hair winter.

Your poems deep in my green coat pocket
sliding a token into silver TTC slots.

Years after your death, there are reasons for these
connections

If today I am in love with you, it is a sweeter ride to work
in love with your language of power
your words
pull me up
and out of *That's Holiday* sweaters.

I am more than this smile
And these brittle bones in my mouth.

At 12, I renamed myself, too
cut down on syllables
because I wanted something
to sparkle against
my bland rural landscape.

I don't think about naming anymore
often throw out an alias to throw people off,
throw bodies off my scent
        (a phone number I made up
                on a pack of matches).

I have a sidelong confident glare when my heart breaks,
In this rush-hour I am replacing her with your words
writing letters to you and clutching my own roses to
my breasts
thorns that fit smooth into crevices
clicking shut, satisfied.

All for you, today.

Drag Queen Maid of Honour

Walking you to the altar
I remember the possibility of being young
The comfort in being close to peril, dipping in just so
And laugh as the baddest girl
births the most Christian middle-class adulthood

Leading the wedding procession
I walk under a sign that reads
"abortion kills a beating heart"
eccentric lesbian maid of honour
wincing, doe-eyed

You were the girl
stared at hard
daring to stare back
teenage best friends
you taught me
How to look boys in the eye
sweet and unthreatening
and still throw a mean punch
Where to get the morning-after pill
and the best 7-inch records
How to laugh
while swallowing surgical steel jewelry
on mushrooms

Sharp on your stomach
your 18th birthday tattoo
a box of flowers

When the priest starts to talk
I watch the outline of your tattoo
under the neckline of your dress
you hide your differences
with soft fabric

I watch the handsome man you're marrying
look at you with adoration
And even my cynical heart
swoons
thinks of a girl at home
I finger her ring lightly
under church lights

A girl who will never stand like this
in front of my aunts and uncles
accept toasters and beer and cheques
teary-eyed glances

A girl who stands in front of me
everyday
in more important ways

I don't want this validation
but the honeymoon brochures
and sweet icing cake
sure look nice

Cut the Pickle

Neil Young songs on ukuleles
Homemade pizzas and
Pyjamas with red feet
On farmhouse floors that creak and whine

My Dad is 33
His cast of imaginary characters
George, Penny and Puff
Three kids who adventured
On treasure islands
"Tell me about the time when..."
And off he'd go to the pretend place
Only *my* dad would go

8 years old in the blue Ford truck
On the way to the butcher shop on rural route 3
The sounds of hooves on metal in the back
The radio singing *video killed the radio star*
At the shop he buys me sweaty vending machine
peanuts
And explains the circle of life
Through swirls of cows dying around us
The smell of blood
And barbeque peanuts
From the sweaty dispenser

Outside, my rubber boots
Kick the mudflaps of semi-trucks
Kick at the ways of the world
My dad shrugs, shyly smiling
Lets contradictions lie

My Private Ontario

I'm a sure shot pool break
strong flirt
with a weak follow through

The elegant arrival
and early escape
out the back
pepper spray
in my fist
on a Hello-Kitty key chain

I'm 8 cokes in a row
heart in the lead
head trailing behind
memorizing lines
"Don't say too much"

I'm 7 martinis in a tutu
holding impromptu dance contests
in the canned goods aisle

A winter, a secret fall
a page 82 medium in the Sears catalogue
pushing cuticles back

In love with the girl
with the itchy arms
who smokes Lucky 7's

Humming "I'm so bored I'm drinking bleach"
racking up the table
I'm my own target

Tits forward
chalking up tips
licking my lips

Two stops away
from 8 collision shops
I am my own private Ontario

Suspicious List #1

We smoked cigarettes at 7am
And watched the building next door burn down

Rumour was our landlord
owned the whole block
and was slowly burning it away

That winter we ended up
farther away from ourselves
than we meant to
fate stuck on our lapels
with the force of stickerbook chivalry

6 inches around our middles
no money thinness
bras made from police caution tape
rubbing nipples against black lighting
human girls as television substitutes
whispering salt of the earth
poems to each other
mid shift

Silly grins eating burnt homemade cookies
writing suspicious to-do lists
mason jars of pennies labeled
Getaway Car

Sweet Bell Peppers and New Order's Greatest Hits

I'm holding the cat
the jealous white dog at your feet
barks like she's going for
the loudest dog championship

We're making the one dinner
I make all the time
I'm loving you harder every day
and fighting
the expectation of ruin
or relinquishing
to love, cherish, own

I thought of celebrating our permanence
fingering the handmade ring on my left hand
the one that smells like sweet lime pepper
two teaspoons curry
crushed red pepper
two cans of pop
sweet sofa date perfection
We are made of money free entertainment
passion.

And what is it now
when our struggle
is only for less struggle

and we can mold ourselves to
goals
see past twenty-five
see it all woven together

Now, in our comfort
why doesn't my arm fit
under your back as I sleep
why am I arched against the wall
waking in nightmares
watching your chest rise and fall

Inventory

The muse just

Caught
Lying on a 20 lb bag
of basmati rice
in the stock room
writing poetry
instead of counting out order

The muse just smacked

Boss rolls her eyes
and scolds me like
the small child
she often mistakes me for
5' tall and wide-eyed

The muse just smacked me

I crumple the poem
in my apron pocket

The muse just smacked me down
between the barley and the powdered milk.

Anti-Manifesto

Kissing with the lesbian avengers, my skull against the cold steel body of Jacques Cartier's statue, head in the crotch of a colonialist hero, girl tongue in mine, CBC cameras catching our pink faces. Lip locked, short and sharp.

The red of my blood used to rise to skin more obviously, in radiation suits in my high school cafeteria protesting styrofoam, those romantic early 90s daydream in Clayoquot Sound, my red fishnets protesting street sweeps in Montreal, my heartfelt rage to Rock for Choice at 17.

I was more adamant, I was spray paint and roof-hopping, sidewalks and silly police. Someone once told me there's nothing more unattractive than an aging anarchist, no one fights the same fight with same fervour without finding themselves out of breath in the corner of some bar thinking, kill yourself or find a hobby, find somewhere to exhale.

That's the way it goes. The way it goes, I fell into the gap, I'm cashing back in. Want to be away from danger, from the personal is political to what's actually possible. Like Ange said, "fuck the revolution, I want

to play video games. I like that one Eminem song." My hand cups my shaved cunt exhausted, I like the way I feel against my comfort and I don't care.
I don't care.

Ok, I do care. When your eyes widen and you can't focus and it takes more and more to leave the house and it's just Thursday night, in a new city, in a new way, with some new ways to calm down. When doctors give you pills to slow the ups and downs and suddenly you're nothing but even, a level playing field, can't kick too high or low, just walk, like ain't nobody gonna break my stride. Easy to think it's another way to be complacent, but it's just another way to survive. Chewing off your lipstick, ripping at your skin.
Breathing is key. Exhale.

When there's nothing to lose you're not out there fighting something bigger, you're fighting to keep it all stitched in your skin, a butterwick pattern of faith, that things get better, better with age. Someone once said we could be more dangerous than shotguns, shooting our mouths off, proud and tall.

What do you do with your urge to nest, to purchase, to become a page in the IKEA catalogue, to have families, to be safe?

Shift gears, fly down a hill with only back-pedal brakes, semi-accident wish lists pinned to my sleeve, like I was still shirtless and 19 singing rebel girl, rebel girl, you are the queen of my world.

Three Days Was the Morning

I dreamed I was the bodyguard for the next messiah
But I failed.
I carried his body in an Olivia Newton-John lunch box.
People inquired about my carry-on coffin.
"He was a little man," I'd say
I wake feeling crazy
Inhabit the architecture of my insides
My dream fast and pink.

Sometimes a journey exhausts itself
Even if you don't leave your bed
Sometimes a walk outside is a meal
A good song is sex and work is a nap
and a conversation is prayer.
I need less confinement.

Instead I just draw pictures
That simplify waking life
Pencil line drawings
Me next to Perry Ferrel
As if I'm still 15
And rabid fandom is encouraged.

With thanks to Warren Buckley

Little Fifteen

At 15
I wrote graffiti everywhere
Tampon dispensers
Church pews
Inner thighs
Train station walls

Evidence of things I'd touched
Maps of who I was
Trails for secret admirers to follow
Proof of a life

Often sharpie high and
Coffee wrecked
I'd tag trails
A taste of criminal notoriety

To see if god was watching

Thanksgiving in Dundas

Hitching the Hamilton highway
styrofoam hot chocolate
from a steeltown diner
waiting, the most precise
measurement of patience

Her building elevator holds
specific movements
the first time I let desire
slip my hand to her neck
lips to mine
palms cupping
the surveillance camera

We are older now
practically married,
she is cooking in her father's kitchen
roasting carrots and yams
home in her fingers

She fought hardest to stay here

I do the shy family shuffle
watching as she holds
sister, brother, father
together like paper valentines

Post-meal, walking exhausted
backseat of smoking cars
I listen as she and her brother talk
unwavering love
the pain of her insight
invisible to the siblings
she protects at any cost

Recognizing violence
she has learned to recognize grace
in others
clear as day over turkey leftovers
drives to the orchard
she holds them together

and her love holds me

Ancient Sauce

Gather ingredients
For an ancient sauce
Drip meaning on my tongue

I am boxed in powdered food
Moulding Wonderbread
Kids roll up in balls
And throw at the ceiling

Add water to me
I'm tepid by the bed
Drunk when hungover
Not thirsty
But warding off death

I want rich flavours
Bright coloured plates
Matching tablecloths
I want to eat the leftovers
and be swallowed whole

Late Night Taxi

To your house
cold fingers on green walls
clean solid furniture
photos of family and me, leaning
into the lens

Ex-girlfriends sleeping over
curious lesbian ritual
pause briefly for the new lover
her things on the bedroom floor

Remember
when letters were sharing
possessions, paper and envelopes
stashed in drawers
a red spiral-bound notebook
a few snapshots
a bus ticket home
I love you scrawled
on a candy wrapper

Passion like running jumps
quieted now to low-grade murmurs
and new longing

Honky Tonk Angels

My mother said to me once that small Quebec towns like ours completely missed the 60's and 70's.

I want to be welcomed back.

I want one corner store and a long clothesline on my wrap-around-the-farm-house porch. To be a speck on the horizon. Sheep to recognize me. Long drives into town, fresh air and crickets instead of sirens. I want to know everyone's name, go to church suppers with prize-winning apple pies, family recipes instead of Subway combos. To come home clean and breathe.

I've always known when you can love.
Time is slow and that's the way it goes.
I walk through Parkdale singing *Honky Tonk Angels*, breathing exhaust, hot around my ankles like cattle breath.

So, When Are You Leaving Toronto?

Montreal breakdancing girls
ragged in the middle of art school degrees
leave me waving goodbye on Bathurst
after two-cheek kisses
and two-week bliss
showing them the town
Canada loves to hate

Saucy in the backseat of a borrowed car
knitting pink legwarmers
along the 401
they laughed at my Toronto life
my high-rent low-glamour ways

When I call home, I wonder
is my dad more disappointed that I'm
a lesbian or living in Toronto?

I pull the covers up to my chin
Settle in
stubbornly.

Summer on Spadina

5 feet tall
and gasping
razor burn and
vanilla talc
cold baths
cool the coals
of our history
the apartment over
the yellow incense shop
accidents that brought us
back together
a brazen Bettie Page impression
not as bold or beautiful
shove my feet into sneakers
shuffle by you
trying to stay
in your shade

The Bitchin' Camaros Greyhound Diary

I remember elk in the streets of Banff and Angie trying to convince us to sleep in an abandoned bus. Vancouver dark and broke and the motorcycle accident on Commercial Drive. Homo Haven in Winnipeg, 3 out of town dykes makes 7 at the bar. Food Not Bombs soup in every city, hands dirty with vegetables forgotten. The Quebecoise lady at dawn in Regina drinking rum stirred with beef jerky. Buying us bottled soda pop. 130 hours on a bus with no results. Just a sore side. The girls who jogged around the bus when it stopped, agitating the cluster of pre-dawn smokers. My head on her lap through the mountains, teaching myself to dream well between rest stops.

In the Wings

Gillian left god
to plan fur store bombings
and break her ties
with fundamentalism

Manic red hair
bloody paint-stained bunny costume
hop hop hop up and down
arms linked, chained to doors
fierce and feverishly fighting
justice a bunny hop down the block
"no compromise for mother earth"
tattooed on her back

As if someday over steak and potatoes
restraining order from the fur district
long expired
she wouldn't look back
and say,

"17? Such convictions"

The Money Shot

I wouldn't have liked to kiss
Jack Kerouac
I don't care that Jimmy Dean
the human ashtray
wrote a poem called
"Ode to a Tijuana Toilet"

They aren't my outlaw heroes

I can't be shocked by the word
cunt in type
descriptions of drunk nights
poet dicks slapping
down on the bar

I've seen a thousand money shots
And it takes more every time

Kerouac spent
most of his life drunk
on his mother's couch
not on the road
to my literary revolution

For Alan Kaufman

Safety Nets

Anna thought the chandeliers were going to fall and pierce our heads. We were 19, at a writer's conference. Fancy Boston Hotel. Not real writers. 'Zine peddlers. Mini-activists. Subsidized and smile selling. Slipping tiny soaps between our feet.
We were go-betweens.
At home giving out condoms and needles, knowing we could lie back in safety nets. Sometimes we knit safety nets for each other out of copper wire and dental floss.

For Anna-Louise Crago

Hard Stares: Brandon, Manitoba

Tell me what the poets are doing
Cause I'm not doing much.
Red earth over my brown boots
overpriced chicken fingers
getting hard stares
city girl in Toronto clothes
with secret rural veins.
Close my eyes and wish for wind
for the sound of forward motion
for the bus driver to wave us
back into our seats.
Sudden shots of memory
like Hockey Night in Canada
in a barely insulated wooden house
2000 miles away.
There's something almost too Canadian
about being in a prairie town
listening to the Tragically Hip
on the radio of a car parked outside the bus station
Gord Downie lyrics like road food
postcards home in the pocket
of a red knapsack
that travelled with your dad.

Shop Talk

Funerals are never like they are on TV
Every death is like another
sitting around in purgatory
talking shop
fidgeting nervously.

Someday this will be years ago

Camp Livingstone

a little jesus never hurt anyone

Pentecostals with shiny sail boats
and horse-clad pamphlets
for cheap summer camp
toured rural schools
parents shrugged and packed

Small cost to crack open
little chest cavities
stick a jesus action figure
in the tree limbs of young aortas

At 10, I enjoyed fundamentalism
why speak in hushed whispers
with your neighbours and cousins
when you can speak in tongues
with kids bused from the city

Returned home
tanned and robust
cherub of goodwill
with obsessive compulsive handwashing rituals
the need to bless each cow
before it went to slaughter

Pentecostals didn't much like Protestants
but at least we could be swayed
They loathed Catholics
which in little Quebec towns
doesn't make you popular
campers crossed their fingers at communion
hoped they weren't going to hell

The pastor (later jailed for something unholy
related to children)
had a son with hidden skateboard magazines
a rebel's edge eager to prove
a face like Kirk Cameron or Ricky Schroeder
minister's sons, always too much to prove
good a reason as any
to read my psalms and pack my suitcase come July
for another year of cult classics.

Red Ink

I'll give you something that'll make you go home and write in your diary in red ink.

Mae West

Pages of white racked with the colour of blood before it dries. Verses about longing, to-do lists undone and laundry piled beside the bed. Calling the cats to cuddle, pulling the covers up, answering your midnight phone call.

You breathe into the receiver, "It takes a lot of trust to do this."

The sound of your name still new on my lips, cools my hot skin through layers of thick cranberry cream and fabric, running through my arm as you touch my shoulder to illustrate a point. A casual gesture, highlight of my afternoon.

Everything is about you. I don't stop pouring red across the page to wonder why.

Greyhound Bus Pass, Midway

Pulled my bleeding hand
Out of my mouth and
Opened my eyes long enough
To see Lake Louise
A braver place I'd never seen
The reflection of it in her
Warm water blue eyes

Low Self-Esteem Versus the Academy

Silly sing-song voice from NYC
a friend says into my voice mail
"I don't want to puke
in a country that's not mine"

Waiting to hear Susan Musgrave
curled into a phone booth
Killing time before the reading
Had a few beers
trying to remake myself
blend into beige lecture hall walls

"Shsh'd" by a brunette girl
in serious brown sweater
university carpeting
thick with meaning

Dreams are made of this
one day I will not
be the sore thumb in the audience
cracking my gum
Scraps of paper poems
falling in waves of misplaced desire
I will read, like this

Biker Bombs On My 21st Birthday

There's no word for the sound a bomb makes. You leaned in to light my cigarette, with the swish of your zippo, I inhaled the explosion four apartments down. Like an elevator plunging and your ears popping and someone walking into you with a lit cigarette, all at the same time. Silly Putty lungs jumping out of your chest.

Burning Down the Main

First summer day
the Miami's back patio
wake performed for winter
Our cold season deaths
come up our throats
fall trickling
down our legs as we squat
to pee precariously
in the dirtiest of bar bathrooms

Megan tosses a cigarette
and keeps talking
caught up in the new birth of ideas
breathless monologues about
a movie we will make
in a town we'll move to
with the girls that will love us
for the stars we'll be

smoke quickens
our conversation thickens
pink tongues wet against the air
smouldering ashes at our feet
oblivious to the wall now certainly on fire
panic

Pour beer and water
over the side of the building
contain it
out as quickly as it came

Kicked out of the bar
we see our friends
moving furniture
in shopping carts
"We're going to Romania!"
they shout.
A Montreal spring for certain;
nothing ever is.

Short Order

Those sultry fast cooks in the back
are trying to win me over
trap the new waitress
with free plates of sweet sauce
I'm an easy taste-tester

You write
watch your back
in oregano leaves

Laughing, I pepper my eggs
try not to look nervous

Homesick Girl

Covered in powdered Tide
the only product that gets out
DNA
washing away yesterday's
scare of the season
lips that kissed the restaurant floor
remembering to breathe
off my meds in secret

Stan's

Outside Stan's store that corners
Barton and Bathurst
With 1982 toys and
Hardened Big League Chew gum
I lock my blue BMX
And sit to avoid falling
Knees to chest
Like an insular incubator baby
Nervous and tight knit

We buy old soda from Stan
Who winks like he's figured out
Which one of us
Is the boy

Femme

The first time I heard the word femme was because of the band Violent Femmes,
and my mother said, "You know what a femme is, eh? The girl in the lesbian relationship."

Sometimes I hear that it means the one who looks straight.
The one who just came out. Fag hag a-politico.
Oppressed by the symbols of her sexual availability.

The day someone said to me, "You know what? You're a femme," I felt at home in my body, in my tall boots, in my swagger and sly smile.

I dig femme history out of the other side of butch, the attached hyphen. Wearing me thin and gauzy, I rip through the fabric myths of my gender. Cherishing feminine pre-stonewall, pre-aids, pre-sisterhood, pre-pansexual queers. She's written as the caretaker, the powerful whore, her femininity making her easy to disregard. A classic oversight.

It is thick with irony that feminism felt it had to rescue the femme. Performing in the same bodies as a way to freedom, assigned gender neutral haircuts, predictable rainbow symbols of mediocrity.

Mixing private and public in my femininity, I define it. The femme and the whore woven together mark a place on the street for the woman who is sexy in her seamless stare, staring defiantly back into the eyes that would degrade her.

for Amber Hollibaugh

Dear Ian Stephens

Deep throating the microphone
Deep February poetry reading
At a little Duluth Street coffee house
In Montreal
The kind of place
you got your own beer
From the half kitchen
In a plastic mug

I was reading for the first time
Ever,
17, scared and wasted
readtoofast
scraping
dirt off my tongue

When you arrived,
Last on the bill
everyone shut-up
we knew we were playing
at reading our diaries
and you were something real
not just because you were dying
I think a lot of us
Thought we were dying too
It was the season of scared

Maybe we were young
And needed someone to look up to
In a literary marvel sense
And you were it
You twisted aids/queer/Montreal specific
Into familiar laughter/anger
Set up stage in fogged picture window
Heat rising from red
and black Warshaw's notebooks
the erotic in eulogies
and possibilities
naïve but learning

If you were still here, would you hate
That we're all so blasé now
Red ribbons at the Academy Awards
And all those anarchist cafes
Closed

Oh, the Places You'll Go!

Grey-haired lady at Bathurst station
Gives me a devilish look and
a *Jesus Saves* pamphlet
On a day when no food
can take away emptiness

I have to brainstorm
ways to save myself

Swallow scotch tape squares
to hold everything
inside me together

People stare:
A girl's unholy relationship
to office supplies

With thanks to Dr. Seuss

Glue and Grain

All I want is
one breakfast
with my girls
reading horoscopes
talking shop and
scraping plates

I burn bleach
into my scalp
in my new kitchen
rapid release of pigment
and passion
press plastic over my head

I want snapshots of coffee
extra toast, homefries well done
shy sneakered feet
under the table
conversations that begin,
"I want to be a good person.
But how?"

I trace their names
in window breath
stir the kettle water
into an instant cereal

swallow my longing
taste the glue and grain

Package breakfast
bleach dripping onto my legs

The Picture Window on Queen and Sorauren

Could tell you some stories
of me and you
split seams in surviving
food, shelter, lonely but for us two
we had it all packed in
15 boxes, unlabeled
18 hour days curled up
riding fists and whipping backs
endless screams and million dollar flicks
we were our own 22 caliber kittens
backdoor betties, prom queen nymphos
City-TV alternatives
to the voyeur neighbors next door

We never meant to be comfortable
so far from danger

I love you harder now that
on train tracks in Banff I hold your eyes
in my dirty pockets and your
trust in my ribcage, locked
wishing you could touch me
on a crowded bus
the timing off, the ride too long
between stops

Cards for Romantic Dilemmas

When you're lonely and someone takes a raging interest – persistent, flowers, dinners, foot massages. And you know in your battle-wrecked yet still nubile young heart, she's not the one.
But you don't care.
Because for all you know maybe that's a myth anyway. You're both smelling sweet and warm and in the moment.
Hearts and candy cards, signed, "you'll do...for now."
Waiting in the wings. Someone Harry met before Sally.

Love's Baby Soft

At 15, these things were sacred: a sweaty mood ring, my ox blood doc martens bought with babysitting money stored in beer bottle piggy banks under the bed, root beer flavored lip gloss, a penny flattened by a train near where I hung out every Friday night with my best friend and a group of guys.

My best friend, a stimulation addict and easily bored, would pretend to get her shoe stuck in the tracks, to test my loyalty. I'd straddle the chain link fence and yell, "Stop fucking around bitch, a train is coming!" Later we'd hug tight, scratching our skin against mini Jesus and Mary Chain buttons.

The next day we'd go thrifting across town with hangovers, chunks of crystal amethysts, old men's suits, polyester prom dresses. Tasting the tongues of butter boys and smelling like *Exclamation*! And *Love's Baby Soft* cologne.

The boys dared us to kiss each other and I'd say, "No fucking way, that's disgusting!" then she'd kiss Missy, who was punker than me, without so much as a shrug.

Caroline Street

The slant of my new ceiling
on the stucco 2nd story
silently casts shadows on my sleeping body
wrapped in green sheets I bought
they matched her bedroom walls

I hold the forty pounds around my middle
that keeps me from dancing
Cherries in the Snow lip prints
on orchard blue pillow case
ripped in three places
open soda cans popping
CD sounds like a phone
ringing downstairs

The bath water drains it's broth
until it is just me
soup bone against ceramic base
shivering my sweltering insecurities
suction cupped, elbows and toes stuck
tile drying
pull a towel over my head
run to bed
stare at the stucco stories
my new slanted ceiling

tells me the stars
have nothing much in store for me
unless I get out of bed.

Mudball

After 7 bourbon sours
I wrote you love letters
On the back of my hand
Until the ink ran out

Love letters
On the roof of my mouth
With my tongue
So I wouldn't forget the words

Makeshift sonnets
On my airline ticket
Somewhere over Arizona
Something witty
To be remembered by
If the plane went down

A sketch of you
Head on my shoulder
Hand on my heart.

On the nape of my neck

Is a four year old bite mark
That resurfaces when it rains
Reminding me of when
You were my religion
Wearing guns and hearts
Around our necks

This isn't stress, it's a shotgun

Soap Lines

Sprint to work
My own half-dressed track meet
Empty stomach

Cut the slabs of soap
spice and wax under my nails
I am caught with the last slice
Dizzy, hot and bruising
Split open on the floor

I lie there and hope for rescue
Until I feel the will
To rescue myself

Back on the stool
At the chopping board
Cut the blocks
Package them
Like nothing happened

All I can think of is thirst
And thanks
I didn't die this time
No one saw me falter
Lose track of production
Time and
Meaning

Basement Apartment

Willy says the one thing she knows
is that something is bigger than all of us
even though we pump up our chests and
heave towards heaven daily

It's dark when we wake
any time, morning, night or middle of dreaming
basement apartment didn't look too bad
in the paper, cheaper, closer together

We've got a pink label maker
everything in the house
wears strips of French
Lavabo, lavabo, lavabo I whisper
fingering the bathtub
shadows drawn around me

Up the stairs
see the stars
with open eyes
seasonal triumph

Is the fast-paced urban world making you stressed?

What if running an errand
felt like meeting a grizzly bear.

This isn't stress, it's a shotgun.
This is 17 heart attacks waking up.
Pulse tap-tap-tapping against the body box
Something shoe shopping and a good cry
can't cure.

My secret.

Autobiography of a Pink Flowered Bedspread

For a while when I was 8, I woke every morning in a cold sweat convinced I would soon be covered in egg-like tumors all over my body.

I kissed Mary Jackson in the playground once and worried this made me gay. All gay people got eggs and died.

Then I kissed Kevin St. Cyr and got over it, not knowing, years later I'd be drawing curtains around beds and arms around me tight. *Proud Life* obituary clippings in my plastic folds of my wallet, beside photo booth snaps of my favorite boys in lipstick.

The Virus Versus Academia II or Why I Dropped Out

The myth of essentialism. Transgressor as knight.
Promethea. Line drawings in lit class I'm always late
for. Twice a drop-out. I meet Trish for breakfast and
I'm too tired to understand things that just flow out of
her. Dizzy students in GAP clothing run around me.
Don't fit in. Little cuts on my fingers. Self help books
and CITY-TV. A blood spurting poet. A pulsating
toddler. I know how self-esteem is bought and broken.
How panic promises poverty. How A. needs to borrow
meds this month cause she can't afford them. My
narrator has fallen asleep waiting for directions. I
ignore history. Don't read before 1978. When can I
eat? Mid-lecture breakdown of protein, syllables, a
notion of feminine writing. 700 characters. 2 pairs of
shoes. Multisexuality. Maybe Promethea just is. Too
strong. Notes in my margins. My first butch-dyke
professor has a scar on her left arm. I stare too hard.
Later that year I see her on Church street at 3 am.
This is my chance, but I don't take it. Politics is a
country of women, she is uninterested.

Separate Bodies

Moment of truth
In an elementary school gym
Anxious behind the man who smells
Like street vendor relish

My mother raised me
Good and scared of sovereignty
I fell in love with you and your
Love of many separations
I want to advocate the downfall of society
But not when my mother is
Alone and scared

Montreal will riot for Guns N' Roses
Rocket Richard and
The Stanley Cup
For punk rock kids who can't bring
Their own beer into a bar
But the future of la belle province?
We stay home, eh?
We watch out the window onto
St. Dominique; it's quiet

Non means I'm a fascist to you
And a revolutionary to my mother
Oui means I'm a good heart to you
Traitor to my mother

Post-vote sleepy
Rubbing ourselves warm
X'ing my fingers between your breasts

Whatever happens
We're still poor. You're still crazy.
We'll still wake up bored and cold
To the creditor's call, at 8am.

Riverdale Snow Globe

Stop staring

On my way home
After performing
Hot lights, ambivalent audience
Eyes like half-warm gravy
My body instant potatoes

It's snowing
on the first day of spring
texture is hard and fake

like I'm standing
inside a snow globe

Somewhere,
someone is laughing
shaking me and the 18 blocks around me
placing us on a shelf
my little life
contained, going nowhere

just up and down in

some sweaty guy's palm

somedays, some girls are
found objects

other people's sticky art projects
Queen Street East accidental floor shows

stop staring

Night shift, light bright

I dream about a city
From the window of the train
She's not waving, but
Certainly staring hard

> *On hold,*
> *a voice assures me*
> *I am next in line between*
> *spurts of Heart's greatest hits*

I have a nagging suspicion
I won't get rid of her so easy

No, thank *you* for holding

Click tapping away
A fantasy that she will
Come up behind me
Kiss my neck and
Stretch her palms
Under my arms that still type
Pulling out each breast
Teasing me into

> *Due to a high volume of callers,*
> *We ask that you please continue to hold*

A state not encouraged by office staff
One hand twisting my
Nipple
Biting my neck, other hand
Down my back
Tracing letters

Tous nos agents sont présentement occupé

Soft breathing on my ear
Words that make me wonder
How I will last until
Punching out
Her fingers and her body
Burning mine

Dear Kurt Cobain

Station Ten, the bar where you could be
17, know five powerchords
And be special anyhow

It was Friday
The singer began to cry
Told us you had killed yourself
Then launched into the first chords of "Rape Me"
I think Jason and I cried too
He looked a little like you
Or maybe tried too hard
When I looked at your photo on
The cover of *Rolling Stone*
I imagined you smelled better
Than he did

We tried to be outlaw rockers
Teenage wasteland style
Also too hard

When I met Jason he was still
A murder suspect
"He's not a typical killer"
says the prosecuter
on Law and Order,
we watched every day

at 7pm
but if he kills,
isn't that typical?

I believed him to be above suspicion
We got high and watched the
surgery channel, and Courtney
reading the suicide note
to crowds of mourners
I wondered if you were pissed off
if you loved her
if you loved
the way you think that you know someone
through your TV

Certain I could tell
good from evil
In that way you take risks
At 17
Sugary and with a shrug
Armful of records

They found the real killer
And Jason was always
A little off
From then on

Sometimes, I wonder
If you'd be pushing out
Endless greatest hits albums
And if kids today
Would think you were a sellout

Oven Baby

My great aunt Olive
aka the oven-baby
was born premature, in 1912

They popped her in a bread pan
low-grade heat in the wood stove
She lived till 99, with a resilient smile

I was born in my mother's 5th month
did my time in incubators
pre-verbal "please god save me" mantras
before I hit the one year mark

The *Sherbrooke Record* read
"Baby with one in a thousand chance of living"
1976, farmer's daughter miracle

When my life circles round the same block
I calm
Not so small against familiar
walls warm like comfort
long to-do lists of dreams
thinking
if I ever get off this couch
I'll be unstoppable

The Only Thing I Have in Common With Ally McBeal

You can't very well proclaim,
with body language or otherwise,
that you're a laid back person
who cares mostly about homelessness
or Ally McBeal,
if you're persistently
re-checking your stove to make sure it's off.
Nervous habits give away my lies.

Entertainment Tonight calls panic disorder
the new "in" disease
I don't feel any better knowing
it's me and Calista Flockheart
painting our nails in front of the TV
more afraid of the sky
than the malevolent eyes of John Tesh.

On the Road, Too Long

Angie, like my cat,
is afraid of starving
her pantry is a bomb shelter
her heart a storage safe

Sometimes she pales
mid-meal,
if she thinks she'll still be hungry
when finished

We traveled across Canada on a bus,
(And if you're wise, you won't ever do that)
Landlocked in the prairies
with long-fingered farm boys
$30 Calgary to Toronto

A middle-aged French Canadian woman
smelling like a mom
filled our empty pop bottles with rum
Regina, 8am
plastic bottled tumblers

Angie, like me, is afraid of being stuck
with people throwing up
we memorize each exit sign
curl up in the overhead compartments
humming make-shift lullabies

Dry heaving dreams in Sudbury
no one likes the taste of nickel
stuck metal tongues
scratchy orange bus seats

We'll call this story,
On the Road: Too Long

$2.99 Coffee included

Springtime revelations falling on me.
In my left pocket, a long-neck glass bottle of Pepsi.
My heart as hard as a hailstone.
I am loved well.

Today, I Did Not Wake Up With Malaria

My neck hurts.
I think I'm dying.
If I said I felt bone weary,
I'd be lying.
My bones are floating
under heaps of skin
forgetting to do their very skeletal best.
Losing weight against blood
I am jelly and exhaust fumes,
scattered bits
of memory and fabric.

Stiff Little Fingers

Out of boredom, I was in love with the boy who sold drugs in the parkette across the street from my first apartment.

He worked at the graveyard on Mount Royal. Wore human bones around his neck. He smelled like I imagined a rock star would: gamey and gross but in a sexy way.

"You know, like, it's not your final resting place. If you're family doesn't pay up, you're outta there to make room for more paying customers."

He sees bodies every day. No wonder he never calls his mother, has a heroin "situation," that look, that smell. At my telemarketing job I think about his long human fingers cupping my shoulders, his greying lips kissing mine.

After a month he topped my earthy pile of loser ex-boyfriends. He called too much. Owed me money. Probably stole my bike. The cherry one with the skull and crossbones stickers.

People say he's in jail, rapping his knuckles against the iron bars, scrapping skin. Thinking of me, maybe, wearing his old plaid shirts to paint my new apartment. Looking for another guy who takes himself too seriously, or just takes too much.

I love the addicts, they'll never put me first. A piece of a pie; in the grand scheme of things, I will only ever be a slice. Always out of reach. My own fingers, out of his.

Don't Watch the X-Files (When You're Premenstrual)

There's something wrong with my liver. I've been thinking that all day and it's not until I wrote it down, that I considered the first line of *Notes from Underground*. The first time I read it, I was also reading the DSM manual and diagnosing myself on the half hour.

There's a pain in the small of my back. My skin is less peach and more yellow-cream. It's the blue office lights. The water from Lake Ontario. That feeling I used to only get from Snowdon subway station; rat hole tunnels and three inches between you and the electric tracks.

I'm watching Yonge turn to Sherbourne, Sherbourne to Castle Frank, short distances, endless tunnels of white noise on hot skin. Pape Station. Read more, concentrate on the mysterious red cut on my arm, think less about the tobacco disease on Fox Mulder's hand, exploding with blood.

Special

You and I were lovers
when I risked death daily
for minimum wage.
Was it you who said
nothing temporary
is ever truly painful?

Looking for Alison

My sister, sort of, she
Lived across from the breakfast place
Said, "I do nothing with my days"
In this city, neither do I
So we made things on her porch
Crafting corners

Every few years
I'm looking for Alison
Our lives run parallel
We always have something
For each other

We pretended to get married
At Church camp when we were 16
Scandalous! The parents said
And we lead the bedtime prayers
Silently wondering how
We got to be in the wilderness
Upholding the word of the lord
When we could hardly hold up
Our hearts and heads and
Our disdain for most things
We think he created

Now I see
Meaning in those simple refrains
Boathouse singing
Kids holding hands around campfires

Looking for Alison
Hoping she's somewhere
Singing some silly camp song
And smiling

Agoraphobic on Tour, 1998

I make a lousy traveler.
I wouldn't mind it so much
if I didn't feel like running away
with my own rambling road show
all the damn time.

We're in the Rocky Mountains
and she's stroking my hair, lovingly.
Crying, tears of disorientation.
"You'll be there soon," she says
and she doesn't mean Vancouver.

I'm a wanderlusty shut-in,
rusting yet raring to go.
A defunct starter pistol.
Pink and brave contradiction
stick me in the trunk and drive away.

Je me souviens

Lemon Gin and Guts

Every day I thank God
I'm never going to be 14 again
Though sometimes I still feel it

In 1992, lemon gin
And guts made me walk across
Train bridges
Into grassy lots where 40's were
Five bucks
Boys cracked codeine capsules
On the knees of my jeans
Licorice lip candy

No one writes about those
Years between 12 and 18
As they are: uprooted
I find no authenticity in
My voice so strained, questioning
I remember:
Bodies not worth their weight
In change for the pool table
I thought that was a regular
Thursday afternoon.

1999, teenagers in packs
At Ossington Station

My adult head pounding
I scoff, they're so violent
Arrogant, morally questionable
    As if I was never
    Able to scream across train tracks
    Entitled to push
    The volume metre of adults

    Harsh and sexy in kilts and high socks
    New hard-ons escaping baggy pants
    Walkmans rung around the necks

    I stare as if I can't even begin to know
    What it's about
    As if I went from 8 to 25
    Without stepping on a crack
    That broke my mother's back

Dear Sylvia Plath

The blood jet is poetry; there is no stopping it
I scribble with my finger those words into the red
thread seat.
In transit, perpetually, watching a 12 year old
Reading *The Bell Jar*, tattered
When I'm stunned in the usual bleeding agony.
The thick, red rush of words in ridiculous moments,
I wonder how it got so
You wanted to be just another offering to the sea.

Richmond County Fair Sociology of Pop Music

The year everyone dressed up as the Material Girl
I was Cyndi Lauper
"The REAL musician" I hissed
Indignant snooty child musicphile
"Besides, she sold out after 'Lucky Star'"

In the corner pizza parlour
After a day of cotton candy and beer
My family comes to blows
Over the last juke box selection
It's a toss up between
Olivia Newton-John's "Physical"
And some song by Dire Straits

My dad insists Dire Straits are the real musicians
He is rallying against the synth-pop centred 80's
My mother pipes in his choice is sexist
My brother asks what "that little faggot has his own
jet airplane" means

My father chooses *Queen of Hearts* instead
And we all mouth the words

Fleming, Saskatchewan

Canada's smallest town
A sign scrawled "GUNS →"
On the side of the highway
A white farmhouse
I wake you up to describe it
You say,
"Did you ever really think you'd ever see this far
ahead?"
The lightening yards away
Is actually 50 miles
A landlocked aquarium.
We confirm, slightly shaken,
we are coastal girls.

Sugar Makes Me Want

We walk down Bloor street hand in hand.
"Jesus was an all or nothing kind of guy," a man says
Our date means treats and walking to the video store
Sugar makes me want salt makes me want sugar

End of a relationship silence
Fluorescent lights and Sissy Spacek movies
You're wearing a thick X-ray apron
Giving up on getting anything else out of me

Low blood sugar on blue bicycles
Fingers trace your face
We know how to get each other
Through strange spaces

Lipsmack, Cherry Blossom

My first boyfriend was in jail
And I was late for homeroom
Smoking cigarettes, drinking coffee
crying into steam

I looked to my friend for sympathy
the boy who taught me about uprising
And the evils of capitalism
He said, "Don't be stupid.
He knew the risk he was taking."

I bit my lip, blood stuck
to my cigarette
Cold coffee, sunk stomach

Wanting *some* boy to say sorry
for waking up underneath
blurry eyed and boots half off
for the expendability of my body

I talked sexual conquests
with the girls
Nothing sacred, numbered lists of boys names
free clinic during math class

Unbattled scars of suburban boredom
little victories
late for homeroom

My Charlie Salinger

In our basement apartment
I never combed my hair
Just kept bleaching

We watched *Party Of Five* re-runs
about Charlie,
handsome caretaker
and his wispy blond Kirsten

If I made it to buy
Vegetables on Bloor
I was proud and slept
Solid against your frame

My spine rubber against you
Listening to the Thing
Trying to chew through the wiring
that died, between the drywall

That spring we protected each other
With armour and pocket change
Sitting at breakfast
Sliding sweating hands over
Plasticized menus at the Black Rooster on Bathurst
Willing Ange's beeper won't go off
Until she's done her food

The plate arrives, and it beeps
She has to go play dress-up across town
for big bucks

We butter her toast and miss her
Wish words could soothe her without
Sounding like we don't believe
she's strong enough

Because no one is stronger than Ange
and my Charlie Salinger

Small p panic

A drink of water.   A pair of cherry converse. As if nothing really happened. She succumbed while daydreaming. Stare at the tall, thin girl in the blue dress at Downsview. She doesn't want a new dress but a new body. From a thought like that to a shotgun round of self-loathing. Distill the emotional contents of falling off a cliff. Take that rush and shoot it in her arm while on her way to class, any ordinary day. Sounds almost fun in print. Like the last two minutes she wasn't waiting out the last few seconds of a full frontal collision. Ten minutes late for class. Wanting that blue dress. A drink of water.

Crushing

Across the table
you're looking right into me
right into my plate
where I wish to divert my attention
from wanting you
to wanting more
balsamic vinegar

This want isn't leaving
stuck in our clumsy embrace

In the bathroom I check
my hair
teeth
temperature
casual gaze

Sturdy boots take me back up the stairs
Certain to keep my desire in check
Keep it off the table
like hardened terror
Bronzed scars and hearts

Feeling something close to ridiculous adoration
one plate of feta olive pasta and
one platter of shared taco salad

warmed, obvious, silly
like a red construction paper valentine
pulled from between my breasts
while you stare

Paste under my nails
knuckles worn rough
joy like a silver stick on star
against white paper to signify
No matter how hard I shift my gaze
to stop the forward motion
17 inches of space between our lips
seems endless

I hail a cab, quickly
before I stumble towards you
and there's nothing left
to anticipate

You know what makes me happy

I'm on lunch
all the fags at my work
are talking about their newest all-air diet,
and I feel a little, well,
out of shape.

Walking down Church Street
I see them, you've probably
seen them, too.
The girls with the big butts
and chubby stomachs
who strut past the gym queens
in their cowboy hats
proudly chubby chicks
sporting tattoos on their non-biceps
standing all sexy
like they own
the fucking world.

Ten Minute Friend

On the side of her record player
a sticker says
"Stonewall was a Riot Not a Brand Name"
She gave me a silver gun as thin as my longest finger
Over her last breakfast
Of God-Like Potatoes at Pins Pizza
On Parc Avenue
Tomato sticky with oregano

She and I played hangman on the
Paper placemats
She spelled out
"You Will Never be the Same"
Throwing out her last breath
Like honey or
thoughtless flattery

You Accompany Me

northbound
5 cuticle moon tattoos
in your strong forearm
by Downsview station
exposing therapy for my fear
of rush hour of blood-rushing

later at the apartment
we take ativan and do housework
tantric dishwashing

dissolving
under each other

years later
you say you remember being taken care of
even while you held my frightened hand
you were loved well.

Niagara Falls Bikini Line-Up

In the whirlpool
Honeymoon Hotel bathtub
She shaves off my pubic hair
And in the mirror
Smoothing Tea-Tree lotion circular
I am undecided:
Prepped for surgery or
Sexy?
I have begun to erase certain worlds.
There is no hair to
Signal the beginning or end of
Me.
Half forgotten
I recede in time
Hide myself in starkness,
Camouflage of pale skin
Bare against anonymous
Hotel chrome and tile.

No Revelation

Deep blue jeans
Breath drawn in quick shots
Popping out of low expectations
in a lower cut shirt

Once I wrote on a bar napkin
"I am more than the stupid and desperate things
 I've done to become less stupid and desperate."

Everything lacks glamour in retrospect.

Angela Cooks with Kale

Dark green into red sauce
wonder vegetables
in her long white kitchen

I complain
that I miss her
as if she
isn't right here

We are uneasy
breathing laboured
stomachs twitching
something about pushing
the weight of uncertainty

Kale is a wonder food
She misses me, too

Writers Should Never Date

In a move of sheer faith
I erase all her voice mail messages
Saved feeling sentimental
Before I stopped myself mid-tumble

Her sweet neurotic ramblings
And cute details
I press 7 after each, "well, okay, goodbye"
Delete her worth to me

Just another writer I admired
At the next table
Eyes as sexy
As my darkest dreams

My 16ᵗʰ Move

When the trains go by at 3am
I'm not sleeping but trying
frustratingly animate
kicking dirty feet against
boxes in my 16ᵗʰ bedroom
pressing the ball of foot to the wall and screaming
I should be settled by now

Naked, I wash the tile floor
pour white Comet powder into bare hands
wet to green paste
dissolve my fingerprints
for deep soul cleansing
instead
I get blood-cracked fingertips
odd, stabbing pains

Back in bed, I
sleep on my back
So my dreams can only go in one direction
can't nest half-flavoured
in my mattress
for years.

Mission and 21st

Only Happy When It Rains
reminds me of Chloë
in a Mission thrift store, San Francisco
deciding which pink ball gown
complemented my combat boots

Now she has two kids under three
and a husband.
She's coming to visit on Thursday
I'm miles away, doing the urban queer
not-easily-explained-to-relatives thing

She says I'm brave to live the way I do
I'm unsure, over her son's crib,
something so cliché and peaceful
about the way his sleep makes me feel
I think about her valor

and the timelessness of friendship

No Cokes For the Whole World

I had a bicycle, a scrappy red BMX with peddle-backwards brakes. I drove out my winter sadness down the Christie hill, listening to sappy am radio. It was the first day of spring, the first day I could tell when my feet would hit the ground before they surprised me. I'd spent January watching Canadian TV teen shows and eating powdered food. Sadness even my true love couldn't cure.

She held my hand on 24 hour fever watch. Talking about going crazy like we were standing beside the track, watching it go by.

What do you say to someone who saves your life?

Sparing Change

Feeding the metre
Leaning the iron box
Into my chest as it heaves
Turn the knob
From violation to paid

In theory, this
Terror is not rational

On Tuesday, it is life
And death in every decision
Parking metre or not
Locking her car door
Tender calf muscles
I search every fold and stitch line
For more quarters
Pressing lips to slate
Grey parking metre
Kissing disease

A moment
Blends blankly into
Hours

I love to watch her paint

She carefully eyes the surface of the wall in her stained white "wife beater" tank top, bracing the ladder. Radiant in her unusual lack of shyness. She pays attention to detail and process, balancing herself on the precarious step ladder. A beer close by. The brown glass reflecting the light inside her and the satisfying smell of a new home. She relaxes into brush strokes. Dips the edger into the paint tray and breathes, deep. She can see where things begin and end. When she spills she laughs, her strength and calm holding up the wall. There isn't anything that can't be washed away.

A new bright clean she can rub up against and leave her own fingerprints.

It's like watching her dance.

Suspicious List #2

3 girls
getaway car
cold cola
solid food
armour
bottled gods

ZOE WHITTALL spent her childhood in South Durham, Quebec, her adolescence in Montreal and the last five years in Toronto. In Montreal, she was actively involved in the spoken word scene, organizing a literary and music event for women called *Girlspit*. In Toronto, she organized *Live, Action, Ladies* and more recently the *PowerFemme* 2001 Cabaret. Her first film, *One Stuck Muffy* was screened at the Art Dyke 2001 competition at the Images Festival of Independent Film and Video. She has performed at Toronto's *Strange Sisters*, *Cheap Queers*, *Sisterspit* in San Francisco and as a guest with the *Wasted Motel Tour* in New York. She's been published in *Turbo Chicks: Talking Young Feminisms* (Sumach, 2001), *She's Gonna Be: Stories, Poems, Life* (McGilligan, 1998) and in the literary journals *Fireweed*, *Index*, *Flux* and the *Queen Street Quarterly*. Her work is forthcoming in *Brazen: Transgressing Femme Identity* (Arsenal) and *Ribsauce* (Vehicule). Zoe Whittall is a music columnist and arts freelancer for *Xtra* magazine.

Acknowledgements

I would like to thank the 1993-95 Poetry Workshops at the Dawson College New School in Montreal, The Fluffy Pagan Echoes, Trish Salah, Buffy Bonanza and Julie Crysler for being so supportive and inspiring to baby poet 'zinesters.

All the writers who have helped me along the way: Anna-Louise Crago, Mariko Tamaki, the Stern Writing Mistresses, Marnie Woodrow, Camilla Gibb, Susan Musgrave and the youth at the Pink Ink Writing Workshops.

Thanks to my mom and dad for transcribing my stories and putting them to music before I knew how to write and for always encouraging me to be creative.

Thanks to Maureen Grant for the cover photograph.